Written by a kid just like you!

BY

H.G.SANSOSTRI

Best wishes
H.G. Sansostri

Tiger Publication Limited

First published in 2013 by Tiger Publication Limited
40 St. Peter's Road, Great Yarmouth, NR30 3AA

Editor: C.F. Sansostri

British library cataloging in publication data available

ISBN: 978-0-9926901-0-6

Written by a kid just like you!

BY
H.G. SANSOSTRI

Tiger Publication Limited

To the real Billy's and
Ethan's of this world!
'You're awesome'

INTRODUCTION

Hi, I'm Ethan.

A kid just like you!

I've written this book to try to help you deal with problems and situations that might arise at school. A lot of this 'stuff' has happened to me on my journey through primary school - oh yeah! I forgot to say, my best mate Billy is on board too, he'll appear later on in the book, you certainly won't forget Billy, I promise you

So are you all paying attention? Read on...!

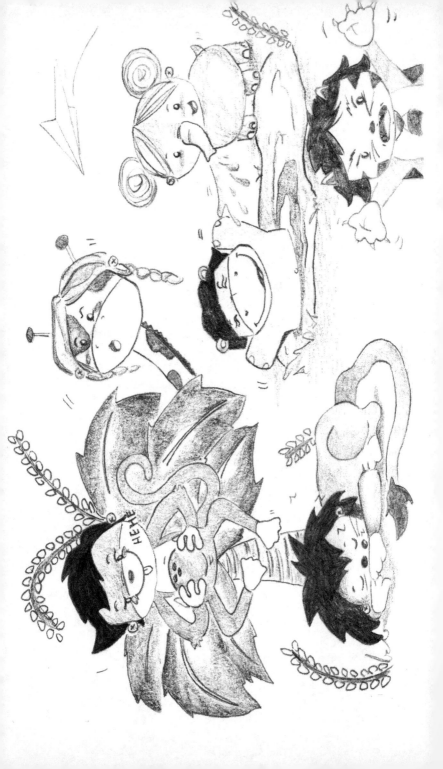

SCHOOL IS A JUNGLE

A big, wide jungle full of wild little animals.
Can you guess who they are? Children!

Children like you and me, running around
sometimes hurting each other, telling each
other off, shouting, screaming and laughing all
at the same time, playing very silly games and
pretending to be monsters.
Of course not all children are naughty; out of
a whole school of children about 75% are nice
and kind whereas the remaining 25% are
naughty, cheeky and very rude.

I would continue, but hey! This is only the
intro.

The next chapter will list the groups of
certain children that inhabit the 'world of
education', from the very start of primary
school to the early years of secondary.

THE SPECIFICS

Not all children are the same, some are naughty and some can be kind. Some are not very smart or intelligent but try very, very hard. There are specific types of children that hang around together or alone so I have come up with an idea that puts us kids into:

'The Specifics'

Here we go, are you ready for this?

The Peacocks

These children are very flashy or trendy
dressers that like to develop their style. They
wear pink chequered tops, stripy scarves,
leather boots, and trilby hats - the relentless
wave of 'must have' clothing goes on and on.

The Mr/Miss Popularities

They walk around school being followed by their crowd of 'popularity disciples' and show off their talents when they can e.g. football, dancing, comedy etc. Those who are hoping to become popular...

Well, I hate to break it to you, but it's not all that it's made out to be. Hmmm (cough, I'll explain later.)

The Outcasts

Those who are treated meanly by others, just because they are too nice or just aren't 'normal'(hey what is normal?).
Don't listen to the 'meanies' because they are wrong. It saddens me and I will continue this later on. They are just the same as you and me, treat them nicely.

13

The Fair Players

Many of these children inhabit the land of education, they play together in groups and the games they play are nice and fair. They stand up for each other and mostly obey the teacher's orders, the right example will always be set by these 'beloved children'.

The Muscles

They are strong, fit and handsome/beautiful children. They are quite often selected to compete in sport competitions and races. I've many friends who are like this, although the ones who are the strongest have focused too much on brawn and not brain.

The Heroes

They are smart, popular, fit, beautiful and
fair.
Very few children possess all these skills and
are truly blessed, but at least one or two in
the school have used their blessings in the
wrong way, by being plain mean to other kids!
The others are heroic legends! I know a few.

Which Specific do you fit into?

Peacocks	Mr/Miss Popularities	Outcasts
☐	✓	☐
Fair Players	Muscles	Heroes
☐	☐	☐

Tick your box

Now, to the Juiciness of Survival!

SURVIVAL TACTICS

As I said, school is a big jungle and is full of
lion cubs!!
Meaning us kids, we are the 'lion cubs', all
playing and play fighting for our positions
within school.
So first we must learn the art of 'Ignoring'
or 'Rising above'.
It's your first day in school and you're
happily walking down the corridor, you've
made new friends today and you can't wait to
hit the hay at home.
"Hey, newbie!" someone yells angrily at you,
you turn around and a red faced bully stands a
few metres away, teasing you and taunting
you.
Whatever you do DON'T RESPOND! They
want attention, if you argue back that gives
them satisfaction and urges them to continue
(don't feed the trolls).

If you ignore them and walk away, they'll lose interest in you as they receive no satisfaction and then they pick on someone else who will crack under the pressure.

It's like my puppy Trickster, if you stroke him too much he wants more attention and if you give him more he'll want more and more and more and so it goes on...

This is primary school so the only insults they should be using are the silly ones like 'dollop-head' or 'idiot.'

If you are really little, try to report them to your nearest teacher or blank them as they just want to try and annoy you!

However if they insult you with swear words and start trying to touch you or poke you - you MUST report them.

If not your unpleasant situation will keep swelling up like a balloon and might become that nasty word 'Bullying'.

NOW THE CLASSROOM

Even the classroom is a potential place for
rudeness.

Let's say you are walking into class and it's
Maths (my favourite subject!).The teacher
says she just needs to go to the stockroom
for a moment. This is where it all starts
because all they need is a moment when the
teacher is out of earshot and "hey dollop!"
someone yells at you, "you're such a weakling!"
Now, in this situation I have personally
experimented in answering back but it rarely
works. You need to be a very quick thinker to
reply and you need to use smart comments as
your weapons, but either you'll be turned on
by 'the cronies' being bully's so called
"friends" in the class or the person you've
replied to will snitch on you. Not fair? I know,
but that's life eh!

I have a certain strategy which works for me
that I have adapted to situations like this, but
it's top secret!

Maybe I'll tell you at the end? (That means
that you've got to read my book) YAY!

Anyway, the basic methods are:

Ignore and someone MAY stand up for you, but if the insult that is thrown at you encourages more kids to join in, try and continue to do your work until the teacher comes back in and then report them. If you return fire with fire you've practically BLOWN IT!

Next is, when you see your friend being ganged up on by maybe the class clowns or even your own friends, don't refuse to report this just because they are your own friends. 'Loyalty' to me is a very important word, I just feel that sometimes my friends need to grow up more to understand the meaning of the word.

I remember when I was bullied by my very own friend Lucas and this kid called Dean who I absolutely hate, sorry, I mean don't like and is another so called 'friend'.

SURVIVAL TACTICS 2

Never and I mean NEVER bully someone!
It isn't just mean, it's a crime!
Bullying is the school language for 'harassing'.
It means that someone keeps bothering you
and they just won't stop.
Changing the tide! You're bullied?
Let's say if someone was to call you a name
and after one day you ignore it, the second

day you ignore it, then after the third day you try to ignore it, if this goes on and they keep bullying you-

YOU MUST REPORT IT!

Anyway, back to the situation.

So two of your friends are bullying your best friend, what should you do? Go and tell a teacher, if you interfere you're just throwing yourself into the fire along with your friend. In secondary school, the 'ball' or shall we say 'bully' game changes a little - get my pun

My best advice is:
Don't get caught up in between other kid's fights otherwise you'll be served up on a silver platter with chips to them as well!
Now, I need to tell you why being popular isn't all it seems. This mainly happens in primary school as the teachers aren't as strict as secondary school teachers, well after all we are little people aren't we.
The 'POPULARS' usually take the 'micky' out

of the teachers, this usually happens during French or Geography seeing how they are the most boring subjects - in my opinion anyway! They aren't my favourite personally but they're not the worst either; anyway back to what I was saying, they make fun of other kids which is apparently funny and they talk during class and do stupid things to 'big' themselves up.

Mostly if you've become popular by doing what I've just explained, or just trying to be funny you've done yourself no favours, the others will expect you to be funny all the time, that's hard work eh? You're trying so hard to impress others, you've forgotten what you're at school for!

They would say 'ooh! There's Terrible Tim, go and call him a fathead!' If you do, you'll be drawn into an endless cycle of 'go do this' and 'go and do that!' If you don't, they'll lose interest in you and go find someone else to do their bidding. So you become the 'Class Clown' - bet you're not happy deep down!

Now, we are slowly moving into secondary school just for a bit, so I think it's a good idea to introduce you to the groups that we might find there.

Please do bear in mind, that I've the good fortune (sometimes) to have an older brother who has passed on this 'info' to me from his own personal experience at his High School. These are the following instructions:

No swearing, no chatting, no insults, no fighting, no chewing, no copying, homework on time, no answering the teacher back, no this or no that, **HARSH EH?**

The Nerds

They tend to hang around on their own and
sometimes move around in groups and chat
about their video games,

homework and
school bullies.
This isn't
to be
honest,
the
most
popular
group,
though
to me this
would be the
most popular group,
as these kids are real nice
kids and peacemakers but for them
popularity doesn't matter, all that matters is
that they are happy in the schools they are in.

The Comedians

These kids are the class clowns first, and
popularity kings second. They gain respect
for, as I said, being daft and mucking around
with other kids and
making fun of the
teachers.
They are
usually
followed
by a
swarm
of
kids, who
would love to
be just like them,
now being yourself
is a much harder option
or choice, isn't it? So be yourself and
meanwhile enjoy their show!

The Internet Sensations

They're not literally internet sensations, but
when there's an amazing video that reaches a
certain amount of views it becomes popular
over the internet. That's how it sort of
happens at school, these guys will do
something cool and then everybody knows
about it, here you get the metaphor 'Internet
Sensations' - so many hits and views!!!
Most of them are usually show offs meaning
too big for their boots, oh sorry I meant
school shoes!

Good Solid kids

These are basically Heroes, they are the 'all-rounders' and are pretty much famous throughout school given their solid reputation. They're not only good with the teachers, they're good with the other kids. Nobody would dare to try and hurt these guys. Good stuff eh?

The Weirdos

These children are unfortunately the hotspots for bullies and 'insta-taunts'. Being in this group is a hard one, I have nothing against them, but it is best to not be a loner and try to make some friends, or even better talk to a teacher, never ever feel alone or on your own (there's always a solution remember).

Report the Bullies, Report the Bullies,
Report the Bullies...RTB, RTB RTB RTB

Hey lets have some fun and reverse this
abbreviation
BTR BTR BTR BTR...
Bully Tactical Reserve, Bully Tactical Reserve,
Bully Tactical Reserve, (there's always some
way to have something to remember and help
you out eh? I use the RTB)

ATTEMPTING TO GET ON THE GOOD SIDE OF PEOPLE

First let's try to get on the good side of the teachers! I'll also be demonstrating what happens when you are too annoying or too disrespectful.

I will demonstrate this with a good old fashioned script.

GOOD WAYS

Script 1:

Don't try and be too much of a goody-two shoes because that can annoy the teachers. Also, don't answer every single question they ask, unless they ask you to answer it, give other kids a chance as well, what's important is that YOU know what you know!

Here's an example...

Teacher: Alright class, did anyone revise the 'Macbeth' play by William Shakespeare?'

You: Mister Warthorn! I did!

Teacher: Okay, anyone who did revise, please explain to me a couple of the characters in the play.

(Here you don't reply)

Ted: I know sir! There was Macbeth...

In this scenario, you lie low and give the other kid a chance too, what's important is that you know the answers as well in your head.

Script 2:

If someone tries to talk to you whilst the teacher is talking just ignore them. Otherwise the teacher will see you and tell you off and believe me, the troublemaker just gets away with it! Always!

Teacher: Alright class, write down a short paragraph that will invite...

Fred (whispers): Hey you! (You ignore him and continue to jot down notes.)

Fred: Hey! I'm talking to you! Face this way- (so turn towards him and say, "Fred, be quiet please")

Teacher: James, why are you distracting another pupil whilst they are working? How about you go and distract some other boy in detention after school today!

(KEEP YOUR COOL, head down and carry on writing!)

As you can see, secondary school teachers show barely any mercy. Get caught chewing gum - detention, littering - detention, talking in class - detention. No matter how sorry you are, the teachers will not back down.

Script 3:

If your teacher would like help doing something, don't raise your hand for every single thing that they would like done otherwise it will look like you want to skip class or you're being a 'sucker'(not good for your reputation).

Yet again, this can be annoying for the teacher.

Teacher: Class 7S, can someone take down this box of decorations to the stage in the hall?

(Linda immediately stands up and holds her hand up desperately.)

Linda (desperate to get out of class): Me sir!

Teacher (slightly agitated): Thank you Linda. I also need someone else to take the register to the office please?

Linda: Sir-

Teacher: I asked you to take that down Linda.

Linda: But sir-

Teacher: Don't question me Linda just do it!

(Linda walks out disappointed.)

You (calmly): I will do it sir.

Teacher: Thank you.

(You collect the register and walk out of the English lesson.)

Evidently, when a class discussion takes place over who gets to take the storage boxes to the hall, when they just want to get out of the classroom, the teacher will quickly understand that the kids are just trying to waste time and that they will take forever to do their task. **(Remember they were kids once!)**

BAD WAYS

Script 1:

This script can demonstrate how trying to show off and be a know it all isn't the best way to go with your teacher. If this has happened to you, we are not liable for repairs, damage or insurance (not that relationship insurance exists).

Ready?

Teacher: Okay Class 7S, can someone solve this algebraic problem on the board?

You: I know!

Teacher: Okay, yes, you, please.

You: If A equals nine and the A is next to the 10, that would equal ninety as multiplication signs are omitted in algebra.

Teacher: Correct!

(You gleam with pride and listen to the next question.)

Teacher: Alright. Ted, Solve this long division sum.

You: I know sir!

Teacher (chuckling): That's good, but please give Ted a chance. Anyway-

You: Sir!

Teacher (agitated): Do not interrupt otherwise you can spend your afternoon in detention. Don't answer back!

(You stare at your desk as the teacher babbles on to Ted, meanwhile Ted is getting all confused and agitated, she then also agitated turns back to you.)

Teacher: Alright, now you can answer the question.

You: I can't.

Teacher: I've told you to, so please answer the question?

You (cheekily): I'm not allowed to- answer back!

CLASS GOES-OOOOOOOHHHHHHH!!!

Teacher: Go down to Miss Gerald's class and explain that you have been rude and disrespectful. NOW!

In this situation you were way too desperate to show your understanding, so you end up with a detention - now that went pear shaped didn't it?

Class etiquette (meaning good manners in the classroom) is a very important thing to master but you'll learn that as you move up in your school, just as I'm still doing!

Script 2:

This one shows how joining in with chatter boxes can get you and only YOU into trouble.

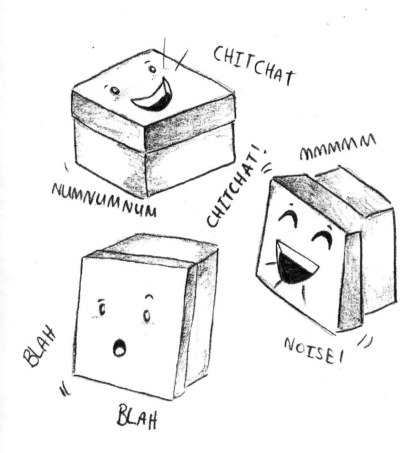

Teacher: Alright, start copying down these...

Tom (whispers): Hey you!

(You turn around.)

You (whisper): What?

Tom: Do you have an Xbox? If you do-

You: No! I'm trying to get on with my-

Teacher: Excuse me?

(You turn around and the teacher stares at you, disappointed.)

Teacher: Are you distracting Tom? He is trying to get on with his work and you are disrespecting our golden rule; no talking in class! (NOT FAIR EH?)

You: Sir-

Teacher: Detention! Do not answer back otherwise you'll have another detention tomorrow.

Now whose fault was that?!
Well that's what happens if you're not careful! All you did here was turn around and interact with Tom, so if others try to talk to you, you must try and get on with your work,

43

otherwise you'll get the heat.

Script 3:

Wanting to go to the toilet a lot will not get you on the good side of a teacher. I should know, in R.E. I used to go to the toilet every now and then to skip bits of the lesson, I was sussed out in a nanobite (hee hee honestly).

Teacher: Can someone please take this box to the office?

Linda and you (stand up): I will!

Linda: No I will!

You: No, I put my hand up first-

Teacher: You two! Calm down. Can you just take it and not make a fuss?

(You stand, stick your tongue out at Linda when the teacher isn't looking, and collect the box.)

Teacher: Now, I need this Charcoal taken down to-

You: Sir! I will-

Teacher (annoyed): I have already given you a task to do, so do it please.

As you can see, even though you want to help, the teacher just wants you to do one thing at a time.

As you can see lots of these scenarios don't go in favour of the kid who really hasn't done much wrong. It's a little unfair, but sometimes life is unfair, it's all about how you handle it.

GETTING ON THE GOOD SIDE OF FRIENDS

Now, when you're trying to get on the good side of a certain kid it's a whole different story from how it was with the teachers.
If they are silly, a 'comedian' or very mean to other kids just don't hang out with them (easy as!!). It makes you one of them- who love to see other kids hurt and humiliated, not cool!

You want to hang out with people who have similar likes and dislikes as you, not someone whose opinions are the complete opposite to yours because that could cause disagreements, and you don't want that.
(I don't anyway!)

Welcome expert No. 2

Billy, hmmm, cough, cough- my mate! So the entertainment starts here!!

E: Shut up Billy.

B: But I want to cause arguments!

E: Oh well, I'm in the middle of a very important conversation with our readers.

B: Yeah, with me!

E: Never mind him, guys, he just needs to be ignored

Now moving on, like I've told you and as I was saying, you need a friend you can trust and a friend who you can rely on, where better to look than your very own early childhood? If you can of course, maybe some of you have moved or changed schools, but if you haven't then get dialling!

MEMORIES

When I was at nursery, I was playing about in the sandpit and another tot walked by and tripped over it, he was crying, tears streaming down and a little bit of blood dribbled down his knee. I stood up and helped him over to the nursery teacher who looked after him. After it was patched up he walked over to me and said 'thank you, my name is Fred.' I still hang out with Fred today and totally trust him!

You see, childhood friends can sometimes form a more solid friendship because you have been with them long enough to know and strengthen that friendship. You're lucky if you have a treasured childhood friend, it doesn't have to be nursery, you can make solid friends throughout your school journey (just be choosy).

YOUR FRIENDS

1) Are they trustworthy?
If they can't be trusted with any of your secrets, they aren't really a trustworthy friend.

2) Are they Rude?
If they are, they aren't treating you with respect (a two way street, by the way) then you shouldn't really bother with them, what's the point of strengthening a one way friendship, when it's eventually going to shatter?

B: Well what's the point of this book?

E: Well, the point of this book is to explain and emphasise how children's personalities, emotions and school can affect you. From a kid's point of view of course (sometimes adults just don't get it).

Do you remember the intro?

'WRITTEN BY A KID LIKE YOU'

B: English please!

E: The point is to tell them how to survive and enjoy school!

B: But isn't it good to be popular? Yes, maybe, this is coming from me, a cool kid if you will, 'Billy the B,' THE MAN WITH THE PLAN! But maybe you look like a total 'goof' in the teachers eyes? What about the other children? Being popular usually decreases the chances of being bullied doesn't it?

E: Well Billy, that's actually a fair point. Yeah... that's what I read in another book called

'How to Be Stupid, Therefore Popular' by Jamie Sydney!

It's a worst-seller and I thought you had changed Billy?

B: I'll never change... MUH HA HA! MWA HA HA HA HA *splutter*...Sorry, I had something in my throat.

E: Let's get back to talking about good friends, I'm enjoying this!

3) If your friend has ever bullied another kid, hurt someone, maybe you should stop hanging around with them so much.

Don't show them that you don't like them anymore, just say 'HI' and 'BYE' no need to be mean and rude.

If you can avoid them do it, but if it looks too obvious don't, just chat to them, leave it there. Or even think of excuses to avoid them, like the following:

DEREK: Hey!

YOU: Yeah Derek? (You say, as you start to walk slowly away!)

DEREK: After school, do you wanna-

YOU: Um, Derek? (walking faster in the other direction :)

DEREK: What?

YOU: I need to go and fill my water bottle. See you later.

DEREK: Okay!

As you can see, simply being polite and busying yourself can change the tide of battle. Whilst you get what you need, they won't wait for you, they'll move on to someone else to annoy. **That's the logic of a child bully!**

SURVIVAL QUIZ

Now, I have trusted my mate Billy to take care of this. If he does anything stupid, I'll take over.

B: Thank you very much! (Billy growls!!)
Now, instead of all this seriousness we can get along to the fun stuff! It's me, yes, me Billy and I'm going to give you a quiz! But it's not just any quiz, it's a survival quiz!
Right, you have to circle the letter of the answer you choose, get 3/5 right and you get a pretty good survival rating!
Get less than that, and you're food for my pet bully Jason.

Are you ready? Let's go...

1) You see your best friend being bullied by teenagers. Should you...

A. Help him

B. Report it

C. Leave him and forget it

2) You see a gang of kids blocking the toilets, and you need to go, do you...

A. Wait

B. Walk straight past them (if you're not bursting of course!!)

C. Or politely ask them to move

3) Your friend tells you a rude joke about someone else, do you...

A. Don't agree with the comment

B. Ignore the comment

C. Laugh at the joke

4) You're playing football and you're tackled by your friend, do you...

A. Call a foul

B. Forget it

C. Argue over the foul

5) You're in a lesson and a kid keeps whispering to you whilst the teacher is talking, do you...

A. Ignore them

B. Tell them to shut up!

C. Engage in a conversation with them

B: I'm going to give you the answers. Remember, you can get a good survival rating if you get more than two right. If not, you're Jason's lunch time snack! Let's get cracking!

E: Get on with it!

Question 1: B!

B: Did you get this right? If you did, well done! Yet again, Jason is hungry... get them wrong! Please get them wrong!

Question 2: B... again!

B: I hope you got this right! Get it? You're writing it down, and write sounds the same as right... and it's... oh forget it. If you went for C or A you need to get the rest

right, otherwise you'll be toast! Get it?
You're gonna be eaten, and you eat toast
so... it's funny because... wow... toast,
hahahaha toast.
I'm toast, you're toast, we're all toast, I
love toast, hmmm cough, No Ethan yet?
woohoo I'm havin me some fun!

Question 3:   What's the answer? It's... B!
B: Wait... what? Three times in a row!
Next thing you know, the next answer is B!
Anyhow, those who didn't get it right are
now wrapped up to be my bully's dinner!
MWA HA HA, HA HA HA! Do you like that
laugh? I've been preparing that laugh-
E: Get on with it!
B: Argh he's back fun's over guys, I'll
take a back seat now! Fine! Jeez, Ethan!
If you have got all the last ones correct,
you are safe, but you can still try for the
best survival rating! If you have only got
two correct so far, you've still got a shot!

Question 4: A

E: Yes! What's a foul between friends?

B: Hurrah! We finally have a different letter! I hope you have written all the answers and why they are the answers – they're the easiest solutions to having a 'chilled out day'.

Now we can move on to the final question. If you've still only got two, you only have one more shot. Let's go.

Question 5:

E: Drumroll please... A! For the second time!

B: Is this really possible? No C's whatsoever? Who organised this answer sequence?

E: Um... YOU Billy..

B: Be quiet. Whoever put together this sequence is a big fat dollop!

E: It was you silly!

B: What?

E: It was you who put it together

B: Oh... fiddlesticks! Okay. So... If you

got the A you got this question right. If not, you have probably been eaten by my bully! Isn't that right, Jassy-Wassy! Oh! Sorry... anyway, let's get onto the survival ratings.

0: *Bully Food*
1: *Rip-apart toy*
2: *Chew toy*
3: *Demolition man*
4: *Survivalist Expert*
5: *Deadly Bully Obliterators (DBO)*

B: If you got 0, you have been packed into a famous can of Hopper's Bully Food, it contains a spoonful of weakness, arrogance, monkeyness and a good portion of clownliness. That is full of Vitamin B for Bully.

If you got 1, you have been stuffed into a big soft toy full of air-heads, dumbos and sawdust brains!

E: That's not very nice!

B: Oh, zip up Ethan! It's better than the way you do it!

E: Oh really? This is coming from the guy who farts his way around town, instead of petrol you use your farts to get around hahahaha!

B: How dare you! So being an 'Idiotus', as

the Greeks would say, is okay but having some fun and making the readers have fun is wrong? Excuse Me??? OWW! That's it Ethan, you dipstick!

E: Wheeze!

B: Ah! My eye!

E: Ouch! My leg!

B: OAFF! That hurt, you brat!

E: Come here, 'Sir farts-a-lot'!

B: Nom on this!

E: Come 'ere!

B: OWW!

E: Gah!

B: Oof! I give in, I give in!

E: Ha! Oh! I forgot you were there! Anyway, let's move onto some true story scenarios that happened to me!

TRUE STORY SCENARIOS

I remember a few months ago, my friend Dylan asked me round, and he said his other friend, Zack, was coming as well. I was okay seeing how I'd never had any problems with Zack, also I had been at school with him for years.

Now, what they didn't tell me was that this absolute... jerk, Henry, was coming too. Now I found this really frustrating because I barely got along with him and if they had bothered to tell me I wouldn't have gone over there ggggrrrrr!

B: So... you find it hard to say words like jerk?

Moving on, well I walked into their house and I was confronted with a surprise (I'm being polite here!) yes, Henry playing on Dylan's X-box.
"Hey Henry" I said politely, and guess what he

did?

He scoffed at me! The silly jerk! I chose to ignore this, and then I watched them all get thrashed by Henry on the X-Box.

"Hey Henry, we never did have that 'one on one' game did we?" I said.

"Well Ethan, we already know the winner." responds Henry (meanwhile I'm containing my frustration and bubbling anger)!

Then guess who laughed with him? Dylan.

In my face.

Right at me.

Not with me.

At me.

Then after that we went to a local Pizza Parlour called 'Da Michele', we went in and this old looking woman served us.

She sat us down and asked us what we wanted, Henry went for Pepperoni Pizza and chips, Dylan ordered Hawaiian Pizza and chips and Zack went for Meat Feast Pizza and a double portion of Chips, I ordered Margherita Pizza, my absolute favourite Pizza in the world, Yum Yum!! Oh yes and some chips!

Well guess what happens next? She asks me again in a disgruntled way, "SO! What are you having?" Okay, so I put on my polite face and I reconfirm "Pizza, yes Margherita Pizza and chips please", and finally she goes running off to her kitchen. When she pops out again she shouts out these orders to us; "no laughing, no shouting, no standing on chairs, no mucking about, no food fights, no fizzy blowing with straws, no running about and no burping! "

Huh? I was freaked out, no joking about with each other? It's not like we stand on chairs or anything, but having no fun and enjoying time with each other. What kind of 'Pizzeria' was this, a victorian one? (oops sorry they didn't have 'Pizzerias' in those times).
We finally got our food, and when we got it we didn't have any cutlery to eat it with, so I thought that she would want us to eat our meals with cutlery, I politely asked her and

she replied shouting back "I'm going to get it." OUCH MY EARS!

B: You eat pizza with cutlery?
E: Shut up Billy! Anyway, back to my story.
I finally got my cutlery and was eating my Pizza, when Henry cracked a really funny joke so I laughed and so did everyone else, but I was the only one to get a cold stare off Michela, was it because I was the only one who hadn't been there before? I don't know though, it's not nice to be not nice. I wasn't quite sure but I definitely didn't like her - YUK!!

Anyway, we went back to Dylan's house and continued playing the X-box game until I felt like I needed some fresh air. So I went out, played in the back garden and cleared my head a little. When I was about to go back in, Henry said to Dylan "Yeah Ethan the 'forever alone' kid." Dylan laughed.
He laughed at me.
Not with me

At me.

B: Not this again!
E: Fine!

I didn't go in and confront them because I think he heard me coming down the hall, he was obviously trying to provoke me so I walked in nice and calm and played with them. He's the kinda kid who uses other kids for back up - just not worth it and I thought you know what, I'm the bigger and better kid here! I have **BRAIN POWER ZAP!**

Though all in all I had a good time because I gave no satisfaction to Henry!

The moral here is 'Rise above mean kids' just as I did!

B: Is it over?

E: Yes Billy, it's over.

B: FINALLY! Though dude, you were smart, the way you dealt with that! I'm proud to be your mate, cough, cough, erm, erm that's enough now!
Do you know that this book could be both funny and cool?

E: No? This book is about how to survive school and that's that! Well...thinking about it, maybe there is a way we can do both, deal?

B: What do you mean?

E: If we worked together, I could do the serious stuff and you could handle all the tests and funny parts?

B: Nice thinking.

E: So what subject are we going to do now?

We're three quarters of a way through this book, but hang on in there and let us entertain you and hopefully help you the best we possibly can.

Remember we're only kids, so our advice is just **THE BEST KIDS' ADVICE WE CAN TRY TO GIVE.**

E: Well Billy lets crack on, hey Billy wake up, wake up you loser!!

E: Well Ethan speaking now, without my sidekick Billy, DUR!! Now of course there is only one subject that can be included at this time. It's...

RAW RATING

Welcome to Raw Rating! Where we rate out of ten the deadliness of each scenario that has been sent in by you!
Let's start, Billy, Billy, WAKE UP will you do the honours?

B: YAWN, STRETCH AND FOCUS, yeah, yeah, groan, yawn, sure thing Ethan.

> Dear Raw Rating,
> I remember one of my friends kicked me in the shin, but it was accidental, I went really mad and kicked him back, was this the right thing to do and what is the deadliness rating of this?
> From Rebecca

B: Pretty extreme, eh Ethan?
E: Sure, right Billy. Rebecca, you should know that violence is never the answer to any problem.
Number one: that could get you into major trouble.

Number two: you should have asked your friend why he did that.

Remember though, it was an accident, so you shouldn't have kicked your friend back?

You just have to put your 'Rise above it' head on.

Deadly rating: Seven out of Ten.

Time to call da da da...Jeremy McKyle!!!

> Dear Raw Rating,
> I was at my friend's house when I heard him talk about me to his sister, and not in a nice way. I haven't invited him round since, talked to him or even gone near him. I would like to know if I was in the right and of course, the deadliness rating of my little problem?
> Jonathan.

E: Now Jonathan, you should try to not show what you're feeling otherwise kids will pick on you more. Try and be as cool as a cucumber (ugh! Do not like cucumbers!) because not inviting him round or not communicating, shows him that he hurt you. Try and act as if all's okay with you and all will be okay with him, things will sort themselves out on their own.

You were in the right, but maybe you over-reacted?

Deadliness rating: Two out of Ten.

E: Alright, last one. Billy?

B: Um...

E: What?

B: Hey look at this...

E: Lemme see...

```
DEAR RAW RATING
I FINK YOU SUC. STOP ANNOYING
PEOPLE WHO WANT TO GET ON WIV
THERE LIVES. TELL BILLY THAT
HE IS STUPID AND HE SHOULD-
```

E: Oh. I see what you mean.

B: Clearly he doesn't know how to spell.

E: Yeah. This is hate mail, how stupid can he get?

Anyway, thank you Roscoe for sending that lovely message in.

You see we give him no satisfaction eh?
IGNORE TOTAL IDIOTS, ITI, ITI, ITI,
ITI!
Let's do another one, for compensation.
B: **Big words WOOHOO.**
E: I'm not using big words.

Dear Raw Rating.
I'm being bullied by a gang of
teenagers at school and they say
they'll beat me up if I tell anyone.
I'm too scared to do anything about
it so I'm paying them with my lunch
money so that they won't beat me
up. What should I do?
Don.

B: HOLY BATMAN!

E: Don, whatever you do, do not listen to them! They're scared of getting into trouble, so they have told you this to shut you up, and you're paying them not to bully you? That is the dumbest thing I have ever heard! No offence but the way you're handling this situation is very very risky.

Report to teacher, Report to parent, Report to headmaster, Report Report Report!

Deadliness rating: Ten out of Ten. Call the Bully Exterminators.

Do you remember how I said maybe I'd tell you the secret to ignoring idiots? Well, seeing how you've read this far I'm gonna tell you and then I'm gonna do another quiz!

B: Another one?

E: Another one. Anyway, this is the code;

IGNORE
TOTAL
IDIOTS

Also known as I.T.I it may be confusing but the special rule is not to pay attention to them aka 'ignore them' so that's the 'ignore' part explained. Then we have the 'total' part and that is pretty obvious it means all, then an idiot is an idiot because maybe they let themselves become one? Though sometimes there is something going on in their lives we don't know about, something not very nice and it's their way of having some attention, any attention, who knows?

B: Like this 'douche' called Richard, who is so stupid and dumb he is - wait for it - YES! Popular. He keeps annoyingly pestering people, just like a mosquito that won't go away and keeps coming back, and all I want to do is, SSSQQQUUUEEELLLCCCHHH!

E: Billy?

B: What? It's called a sound effect.

E: So that is my special code...

IGNORE, TOTAL, IDIOTS   I.T.I

Now, I need to take the dog for a walk so Billy
is gonna fill you in and tell you a true story
that happened to him.

**B: Yep! Don't worry, it's not gonna be
BORING like Ethan's.**

E: Yeah yeah yeah, see ya, see ya, wouldn't
wanna be ya!

B: Bye!

Insult Boxing

B: Alright. I'm not gonna tell you that
rubbish because of two reasons,
ONE, I don't have any stories to tell you
about!
TWO, Ethan is gonna go 'stirfry bonkers'
if I don't tell you about something,
anything!
So instead I have something really exciting
to tell you guys, I have recorded a
commentary with myself and Nicholas
Darrensman.
This commentary is about the sport 'Insult
Boxing' and Liam the Licker's victory...now
we're talking,
Are you ready for this?

Nicholas Darrensman the Commentator...

"Hello ladies and gentlemen,
Welcome to Insult Boxing. A very tense and
hard atmosphere is looming over the audience
today and that is very surprising, usually the

audience go wild, yet still maintaining some dignity (we hope).

Before the game starts, I would like to introduce Billy Watson who is with me commentating for today's game;

Billy what do you think of the match today?"

B: Well, I think Liam the Licker is gonna throw a few awesome insults and send the opponent crying in agony. Anyway, whoever wins really deserves it because they have both got so far.

N: Fair comment, as we can see, 'Liam the Licker' and 'Amazing Aaron' are sitting down in their chairs and giving each other very cold, glacial stares. The referee is talking to his assistant before the match starts up. Billy, who do you think is in favour?

B: Probably Amazing Aaron Nick, he has won several championships and Liam is a newcomer though a strong contender. The crowds are really supporting Aaron which means he is getting more of an adrenaline rush just through having the crowd behind him, so he will pump out those insults even quicker!

N: Fair enough. The referee is talking to the contestants... and the bell has rung! Ooh, that's a pretty hard insult from Liam; 'spot face.' Aaron flinches a bit, but he is still staring at Liam, he has just come back with a 'your mum' cuss that is pretty harsh, I hope

Liam's mother isn't present today...?
OOOOHHHHH, she's over there, looking as
red as a beetroot and puffing herself up so
much she's gonna explode, KABOOM! I hope
she does, YUK!

B: Actually Nicholas,
yes, there is a mad,
raving woman in the
crowd, that's his
mother Elizabeth, she
looks furious and blood
red indeed!

N: Oh no! A tear is just about to find its way
down Liam's face, but he needs two more
tears to dribble down and he will lose!
This is a fierce tear count! Liam has just
thrown down a deadly 'meat paste face'
insult. I think this is what he said: "Hey, no
wonder you're so dumb, meat paste face."

B: That must really break his heart, also
ladies and gentlemen, this sport isn't just
about insulting each other; it's about
testing their durability under pressure, it

81

seems today that there is a very tense
atmosphere.

N: No wonder! Aaron has flinched yet again
and his eyes have turned bloodshot, it's
amazing how much he is actually enduring
those 'slamming' insults from Liam.

B: Absolutely right Nicholas, the endurance
levels of the competitors is absolutely
astonishing. I could never deal with that
amount of pressure.

N: Oh! What has happened here?
It seems Aaron has run out of the arena in
tears!
The referee has walked up to Liam and raised
his arm, and it is over! The crowd are going
berserk, their jaws are hanging wide open in

disbelief.

It's weird, even though he didn't show it, he must have been crumbling on the inside.

So Liam, the underdog has won the 'Grand Insulter Trophy' and we announce that the official winner is...?

Liam the Licker'!

Well done Liam you were mind blowingly AWESOME!

B: Next week John Vatighan and Nicholas Darrensman will be hosting the commentary of the qualifiers at the Derby Open. Thank

you ladies and gentlemen and good night.

B: Yes, me, having a commentary with Nicholas Darrensman! WICKED!!! The number one presenter in the whole of the UK!

I'm way too cool to go to skool. Alright, guys, I can hear Ethan coming in. Remember, I told you a story wasn't it good? Shush now!

E: Hey Billy I'm back, How did it go?

B: It was greeeeaaaaaattttt, wasn't it guys? Shhhh! hee, hee! I shared a special real life story with our readers.

E: Really?

B: Yep and a survival code, wink wink!!

E: Oh, what was the code?

B: Um... Um, cough, erm, oh yeah, I remember now it was... LWTE.

E: LWTE?

B: LAUGH WITH THE ENEMY

It means that if you don't like a certain person, don't show it, 'Hi and bye' them, which says that if someone was to walk up to you, talk to you and you disliked them; you just don't show it. Just treat them like another friend, and maybe one day they will become another friend. Hmmm?

E: That's an awesome code. I actually have a story that is pretty similar to that.
This happened in Primary school...
I was walking home from school with my friend Sam and we were in conversation about school and about SATS tests...

This eventually lead to discussing other pupils and he told me that Klaus was a total geek and that he would never EVER be a cool guy.

Now, Klaus was a good friend of mine and I felt guilty agreeing with him, so I had three options:

Option one I could be disloyal and discuss it even more? As I told you, it would make me feel like I was betraying my friend and that's just not cool with me.

Option two Comment that Klaus is a friend of mine? I could suggest that Sam doesn't talk to me about my friends in that way, though he is free to his opinion.

Option three Go along with it? By going along with him and acting the whole 'you are SO right' character you avoid any hassle.

WHAT WOULD YOU DO?

To avoid this, try not to talk about someone behind their back to someone else.

Number one - They'll probably tell the person that you gossiped about them.

Number two - This could start an argument and the next day probably they'll have enrolled an army of supporters to pick on you.

E: Have you got one?

B: Um... yeah. I remember one time when I was in the lunch hall, my friend Jason was planning on sitting next to me when he stopped and turned to his friend and said "Oh no! It's the guy who plays Pokemon! Don't sit next to him!"

E: That's dumb, you two good friends?

B: Yeah, as I said; L.W.T.E., LAUGH WITH THE ENEMY

E: Right. Don't worry about him, loooooseeeeeeer!

Anyway, we are close to the end but there is still plenty of 'Ethan & Billy's' advice to be given to you.

First off, just to see if you were listening, we're gonna give you a quiz, it's not any ordinary quiz either, because you'll have to choose between L.W.T.E., I.T.I. or even protest.

Believe me this test will really stretch your

Skool Survival Skills!

Question 1;
You're at a party and your friends start
picking on someone...
A. Protest
B. L.W.T.E.
C. I.T.I.

Question 2;
You walk past your friend who is being picked
on by a complete jerk...
A. Protest
B. L.W.T.E.
C. I.T.I.

Question 3;
A kid walks up to you and says that a bigger
kid is bullying him...
A. Protest
B. L.W.T.E.
C. I.T.I.

Question 4;

During an exam, a kid keeps nagging you to turn around...

A. Protest

B. L.W.T.E.

C. I.T.I.

Question 5;

A massive argument is taking place between the girls and boys...

A. Protest

B. L.W.T.E.

C. I.T.I.

E: Alright, those are all the questions. Billy, is Jason hungry?

B: **Yep. Remember, less than three and he'll nom on you like a bone.**

E: That's right, to be honest I don't agree with it but it'll have to do to make sure you do well! Alright, number one...

B: **Question one is... C!**

E: Right. Let me elaborate-

B: **Nerd.**

E: What was that Billy?

B: **Um... a bird! Over there!**

E: What? You can be really weird sometimes. Anyway, protesting against a 'crowd of kids' is pure lunacy as you'll soon be surrounded by them all.

L.W.T.E. means to basically laugh along with them so I don't think that option is really valid for this question.

The right way to deal with this situation is to sit this one out and use...

I.T.I. Ignore Total Idiots, no point in getting yourself picked on as well, if they come up to you asking you why you didn't

stand up for them, show your support, but

bluff it out as well.

B: Question 2 is... A

E: If there is only one bully picking on your friend, you can help them out; unlike the first question. If you were to abandon your friend here, you're not a good and loyal friend.

B: Like you do that for anyone...

E: *SMACK*

B: OW!

Question 3 is... A!

E: If anyone, friend or foe (meaning enemy) walks up to you and says they are being bullied by someone you have to report it. They're obviously telling you and asking you for help, therefore you advise them to report it and even go along with them if that's what they want, what's the point of listening, then going off to play football and forgetting about it, not nice!

B: What happens, if you don't like that person?

E: Listen! 'Friend or Foe' (foe meaning enemy)

yes, yes okay, cool it, I'm repeating myself here! It doesn't matter coz they are asking for your help, anyway don't you know what 'foe' means.

B: Um... It means ENEMY!

E: Hmmmm, I wonder how you came up with that answer?

B: Alright smarty pants! I don't need a definition now!

E: Alright! Sheesh...

B: Question 4 is... C!

E: That's right, if you turn around and confront the kid you'll get into trouble, not them. What you need to do in this situation is keep ignoring them until they quit, get bored, get caught in the act or wait until they turn their attentions onto someone else! (I know poor someone else!) Maybe they could use our survival guide?

B: Question 5 is... C! Again!

E: Yep! If there is a giant war going on between your classmates, just take a back seat, if you try to take sides, you might get heat from the people you didn't side with, or then again that you did side with.

There's no point getting in the crossfire, is there? So that concludes yet another test boys and girls. Hope you enjoyed it. Billy, give the ratings please.

0: **A simple wuss**
1: **Bully Fodder**
2: **Weak resistance**
3: **Survivor**
4: **Street Smart**
5: **Untouchable**

SNITCHING AIN'T COOL!

B: Being a snitch for really really stupid reasons like being told by someone to shut up, will instantly make you a target to all the meanies and bullies, or as I prefer to call them - Jerkies!

E: Anyway, let me tell you how to handle things without resorting to snitching, unless of course you want to be hunted down by the meanies and bullies!

First off, if someone says something like 'you suck at football' just shrug your shoulders and walk off to do something else.

You could also go for the more natural approach and say 'I'm better at other things' and leave them stunned and then they have no comeback. 'Why didn't they argue back?' they'd be thinking.

Who scored the goal there eh? WE DID!

Also, don't go telling other people not to snitch because that's not your business really is it?

EVERY MAN TO HIMSELF!

(I'm sure I've heard that somewhere)

B: Yeah. Just lay low and try not to stick your nose into other peoples business.

RAW RATINGS

E: Welcome back to Raw Ratings! The place where we rate your stories out of ten to see how deadly they are.
Can we have the first one Billy?

B: **Zzzzzz...**
E: Billy?
B: **Zzzzzz...**
E: BILLY!
B: **Ah! What, who, how and why?**
E: Billy, what are you doing?

B: Oh. Sorry, I drifted off during the beginning.
Uh-huh, anyways, yeah yeah, hmm, can we have the first one please? Not understanding a thing here, what's new eh?

> Dear Raw Rating,
> When I was eating lunch, nobody would sit next to me, for some reason, not even my best friends would come within twenty feet of me. I finally realised this all was happening because people are spreading rumours about me having 'The Cheesey Smell.' It makes me very sad.
> What should I do about it?
> Frank

E: Whoa, that is quite...sad?
B: Loner.
E: What?
B: What? I didn't say anything.
E: BILLY??? I'll give you the benefit of the doubt, okay? Moving on to your question

Frank, that is pretty serious and you should tell your parents and report it to the Head Teacher. There is no need to feel alone and sad, you must report this immediately.

Deadliness rating: Seven out of Ten.
Needs Head teacher intervention.

E: Next one Billy!

> *Dear Raw Rating,*
> *Every single time I try to join in a conversation with my friends, they shove me straight out of it. I don't get it, it's as if they think I'm transparent or something?*
> *Nate.*

E: Umm... the good news is that this situation is pretty easy to handle. You only need to do one thing and that is to find someone else to play with. The kids who are being mean - Rise

Above Them. Don't talk to them unless they start to talk to you. Soon they'll be talking to you as if nothing had happened, remember, your being the cool kid here.

Act like nothing has happened otherwise you're the vulnerable one.

Deadliness rating: Two out of ten.
A new wardrobe of friends.

E: Alright. Last one Billy?

Dear Raw Rating,

Since the beginning of Secondary School everybody calls me a 'Nerd' or 'Goldilocks'. It's all because sometimes I can be really smart (Nerd) and yeah, also it doesn't help that I have long, blonde curly hair (Goldilocks) it adds to my 'Nerdness'!! I really don't want to be a snitch but at the same time I need to put something into action, HELP?

William

B: **Wow, he is in a deep amount of 'unpopularity' right now.**

E: This is pretty serious. William, you may not realise it, but they are actually bullying you, and you are starting to feel the pressure, just like a kettle when it gets to its boiling point. You have to report it as it will only get worse. Okay keep your calm, report it and release all that built up pressure and you'll feel much better afterwards.

Ten out of Ten: call the Bully Exterminators.

TRUE STORIES

E: This one is Billy's. He's taking his 'pet bully' to the vets.

He didn't want me look in his diary but I have to tell you about how being with the wrong friends can become a little uncomfortable...

06.09.11
DEAR DIARY,
TODAY I FOUND SOME NEW FRIENDS!
EVEN ON THE FIRST DAY OF SECONDARY
SCHOOL, WHICH I DOUBTED I WOULD
FIND ANYONE. THEIR NAMES ARE
THOMAS, FRANCO, DEAN AND JEROME.
THEY'RE PRETTY COOL FRIENDS AND ARE
REALLY FUNNY, MOSTLY IN THE
CLASSROOM WHEN THEY START
LAUGHING DURING CLASS.
THEY WANT ME TO HANG OUT WITH
THEM THIS WEEKEND!
BILLY

E: Here's the second entry from his diary,
Billy made yet another mistake and got into a
'not nice conversation' with his so called
mates...

07.09.11
DEAR DIARY,
TODAY, ON THE WAY HOME FROM
SCHOOL, WE WERE TALKING ABOUT THE

TEACHERS, WHEN JEROME STARTED
TALKING ABOUT GEORGE, (UGH, NOW
THIS IS GETTING UNCOMFORTABLE)
NOW GEORGE IS A PURE GENIUS WHEN
IT COMES TO MATH AND IS ALSO A
REALLY NICE KID. ANYWAY, THEY
STARTED SAYING HOW MUCH OF A 'GEEK'
HE WAS AND HOW HE COULDN'T THROW
A PUNCH EVEN IF HE TRIED. IT WENT ON
A BIT, I WAS FEELIN LIKE I WANTED TO
BE SOMEWHERE ELSE, ANYWHERE, BUT
NOT HERE WITH THEM RIGHT NOW.
THEN THEY ASKED ME FOR MY OPINION. I
REALLY WANTED TO STAND UP FOR
GEORGE, BUT THESE GUYS WERE MY ONLY
FRIENDS (OR, I REALLY THOUGHT THAT
THEY WERE).
SO I FELT A LITTLE SCARED AND AGREED
WITH THEM.
IT JUST DIDN'T FEEL RIGHT AT ALL AND
I KNOW IT WASN'T THE RIGHT THING
TO DO...
BILLY

After this, it gradually leads into more trouble. This is the next one...

09.09.11
DEAR DIARY,
THE GUYS GOT ME INTO DETENTION!
MY MUM WAS REALLY ANGRY WHEN I GOT BACK HOME.
THIS IS WHAT HAPPENED...
DEAN WHISPERED A JOKE TO ME, I THEN HOWLED WITH LAUGHTER. IT TURNS OUT THAT IF YOU LAUGH DURING CLASS WITH MR. WHISKEY, IT'S INSTANT DETENTION. FOR SOME REASON, MY GUT INSTINCT TELLS ME TO NOT HANG OUT WITH THESE GUYS ANYMORE.

E: Now, you can understand why Billy didn't stop hanging out with them, because he only had them as friends (or he believed that they were his friends).
Poor Billy, whatever happens don't EVER get into the middle of a fight between your friends.

If Billy had chosen his friends wisely all of this wouldn't have happened.

It can be a cruel world out there, between us kids!

The Final Stretch!

That's right guys, it's almost the end of the line. Don't fret though because we have still got three pieces of survival advice left to tell you. So Billy, do you want to... Billy what are you doing?

B: Playing Reloaders - Dual Wield. It's the best game ever!

E: You downloaded a game onto my computer? You're meant to ask me before you do that you Durbrain!

B: Shut up. You're treating me like I'm six years old.

E: You said it Billy, you are six years old!

B: Just... do your 'hickey-talk with compassion thing' for an hour, I dunno!

E: Sorry about that guys, okay let's get started. As you know, I have told you all about the groups of children you might find in primary schools; though I did leave one out, here goes...!

The Jerks

Their special ingredient is 'popularity' but the wrong type, and this is made up of a dose of rudeness, stupidity and dumbness, my words, my words Billy before you start!

For Example
I was having a discussion with Zack on who invented the telephone. So I mentioned Alexander Graham Bell in our conversation, I then said he invented the telephone whereas Zack said 'no it wasn't him', so we got into an arguement about it and I was putting up quite a 'verbal fight' then he goes away and asks for backup from Henry, James, Andrew and George???
Then they started ganging up on me and out of frustration I told Henry to 'ZIP UP' and he threatened to 'SUE ME'
(well I dont know what that means do you?) and take me to court! What a-

B: Jerk.

E: What?

B: A jerk. You find it difficult to say the

word 'jerk' so I said it for you, what a good friend I am!

E: Shut up Billy! Yes, yes point taken, but I didn't run for back-up to discuss this with my friends, I rely on me, and that's what I mean, get it? That's one of the things that can happen in school (especially secondary school). Also remember that communication is the key to solving this. If this keeps happening, you need to communicate to your Mum, Dad, Teacher or Head of Year, but do communicate, whatever is bothering you.

Dumb and Dumber

B: Oh no!

E: What?

B: Um... nothing... it's nothing.

E: What did you...you broke it?

B: Ouch!! It's not my fault your computer dates back to the Stone Age is it?

E: You are so stubborn!

B: You're so stuck up!

E: Moron!

B: Idiot!

E: Computer nerd!

B: How dare you, teachers pet!

E: Why you little... jerk!

B: You think you're so smart. You're the nerd and the stubborn one, all you ever do is talk about how smart you are!
Oh no wait, you are good at one thing; 'sucking at absolutely everything'!

E: Right that's it!

B: OOF!

E: You fix that computer now, or we're both in it, do you get it? Both!

B: Yes Ethan, cool it, okay message received.

E: Dumb and Dumber that's what we are Billy, okay so let's stop it now! Let's move on...

A TROUBLE SHARED IS A TROUBLE HALVED

B: So true.

E: If you feel unhappy or someone is bothering you at school, you can talk to your Mum or someone you trust. You might also sit down with a snack, drink and have a chat about it, or you could play a board game and throw it in with the dice. How you are feeling during the game, or maybe watch a movie (or pretend to) put it on with subtitles and have a chat and offload all those worries!

You'll feel better, trust us - Billy and Ethan.

BEGGING IS A NO NO!

E: Alright guys, we're onto the second part of the Final Stretch.

Billy was gonna do this part and help me out but he has stupidly gone and broken my computer so he can spend the rest of his time fixing it!

Let's move on.

Begging your friends for whatever, is not an option!

Bullies will respond because they know you're a weak target, Jerks will use it to humiliate you and know-it-alls will use it against you.

Here's another example that actually happened to me.

We were playing a lovely game of cricket and we were thrashing the other team when some kid came along and took the ball.

He wouldn't give it back unless we bowed down to him and did what he said. Some kids were considering doing what he said, but I didn't, I walked off to do something else until he got bored and gave us back the ball. Easy as!

It's attention-seeking that's what it is, if you do what they want they'll just be getting fun out of it and won't get bored as they have an audience.

If instead, you just shrug your shoulders and walk off, they'll lose interest and go and do that to someone else who unfortunately will give into them.

E: How's the computer?

B: Um... is the screen meant to go black?

E: What are you doing to it Billy?

B: Nothing. I bet it's just asleep...

E: Honestly Billy!

B: It will wake up at any moment... NOW! Yeah... hate to disappoint you genius but it's still broken.

No! No it isn't, just give me a sec.

E: Back to our conversation.

Begging someone is another way to make yourself vulnerable, a target. You need to lay low and if someone wants you to do something for them, just say NO!

You need to have a strong mind and believe in yourself and then others will believe in you.

This is an added extra...
AN ADDED EXTRA FOR THE GIRLS!

E: So, for the girls, we have a bit of advice...okay, okay wadda we know your askin'? Well we, Billy and Ethan are entitled to our opinions aren't we?

You are a weird species though! Not you Billy, the girls!

B: I didn't say that,you did Ethan!

E: Snitchin now Billy?

B: *Gggggggrrrrrrrrrrrrrgggggggrrrrrrrggggggrrr*, Im gonna explode!!!

Rule one

Watch out for the 'girls in groups' as they can get gossipy, yakity, yak, yak.
Especially girls who are the 'The popularity queens' or 'The fashionista's' they are a whole other ball game.

Rule two

Is that if you like Justin Bieber or One Direction just don't make it obvious!
Keep it to yourself or some of the boys will make fun of you, because they think it's funny or weird to like a popstar.

B: Well it is.

E: What?

B: It is funny because 1D and Justin Bieber are really naf at singing!

E: That explains the reason why you have a Justin Bieber bed sheet and Justin Bieber duvet.

B: Yeah but... it's because, erm, yeah... ITS MY SISTERS!! Oh zip up Ethan!

E: Hey boys, watch out for the girls paired up together as they seem to possess some sort of 'Tractor Light Beam' that drags you into an endless pit of annoyance with their high-pitched giggles

and annoying snotty attitudes.

'THE QUEEN BEE'

B: TRANSLATED - Those girly leaders that all the other girls run after, group around and then listen to commands and gossip of the day, and then, they pamper each other (what's that about?) Honestly, how do they do it? Though not all girls will agree and follow the 'Queen Bee' they choose to 'buzz off' somewhere else, good on 'em! That's what I say eh Ethan?, eh Ethan?, eh Ethan? Ethan?

E: YES BILLY I HEARD YOU THE FIRST TIME!! But well explained mate!

So in total, for all the girls reading this book, hope you liked our observations on 'your species'!

B: Hi girlies, from Billy x

E: Billy, we are putting a book together, not getting distracted!

B: Hmmmm, well just wanted to say 'Hi'

E: Moving on...

Anyway, that's a bit of Ethan and Billy's
'Best We Can Give Advice'
for you girls, from us boys x

Romances

These do go on in primary school, but mostly secondary school.

Well we are bigger kids then, aren't we?

If you do have a romance going on between you and someone else (I do, but Im not telling you so don't reveal it Billy!).

Yes, keep it to yourselves as someone will tell someone and then the fun begins... and maybe you won't be comfortable with the others knowing.

If you're happy with your friends knowing thats also cool, we are all different aren't we? But, my romance is for me and my girl only.

B: Hey Ethan what about me, any girlies out there?

E: No and 'I DON'T CARE' - I sing that song a lot.

B: Its theraputic, theuraputic, theiraputic, Ethan?

E: Billy, T H E R A P E U T I C!!

It 'awake' yet?

B: No, but... give it some more time. You can't rush electronics.

E: It's pointless Billy, I give up with you!

FINALE TA DA...

E & B: Now guys, thank you so much for getting to the very end of our book.

E: We hope that you have enjoyed the bumpy, funny ride, made up of our advice and real adventures.

B: Remember try and use our advice, as we are kids just like yourselves with our...

Every Day Classroom Problems

We may be back with another
adventure on
'How to Survive your Holidays'

or even

'How to Survive Secondary School'
Not one we have discovered as of yet.
Thank you guys and see you later!

B: Wait.. I think the computer's waking up Ethan!

E: Is it? Lemme see!

B: Wait, what does it say here? This computer is overloaded and vulnerable to viruses, emergency self-destruct imminent...

E: Oh Holy C-

KAAABBBOOOMMM!!!

E: *cough* *splurt* Nice one Billy!

B: Thanks pal. *cough* *cough* *splurt*

Author: H.G. Sansostri

Harrison is an 11year old boy, who likes to read and write in his spare time. He has written two books to date and they are: 'The Little Dudes' Skool Survival Guide. 'W.C.P.' (War Changes People) which will be available soon.

He is also an accomplished child actor having appeared in film, commercials and West End Theatre.

He hopes to study law and become an 'Entertainments Lawyer' and study English and history at a university in London, enabling him to continue his acting career.

What doesn't he like...?

Brussel sprouts and Kit Kat bars

What does he like...?

Chocolate and chips :)

Keep in touch with H.G. Sansostri
E-mail: *hgs1709@hotmail.com*
Facebook and twitter: *H.G. Sansostri*